GETTING TO KNOW
THE U.S. PRESIDENTS

M I L L A R D
FILLMORE

THIRTEENTH PRESIDENT
1850 – 1853

WRITTEN AND ILLUSTRATED BY MIKE VENEZIA

CHILDREN'S PRESS®
A DIVISION OF SCHOLASTIC INC.
NEW YORK   TORONTO   LONDON   AUCKLAND   SYDNEY
MEXICO CITY   NEW DELHI   HONG KONG
DANBURY, CONNECTICUT

Reading Consultant: Nanci R. Vargus, Ed.D., Assistant Professor, School of Education, University of Indianapolis

Historical Consultant: Marc J. Selverstone, Ph.D., Assistant Professor, Miller Center of Public Affairs, University of Virginia

Photographs © 2005: Bridgeman Art Library International Ltd., London/New York: 28, 29 (British Museum, London, UK), 20 (Chicago Historical Society, Chicago, USA); Corbis Images: 12 left, 17 (Bettmann), 9 (Gianni Dagli Orti), 7, 14 (Lee Snider/Photo Images); Getty Images/Hulton Archive: 3 (Mathew Brady/MPI), 26 (MPI), 27; Library of Congress: 22; National First Ladies' Library: 18; North Wind Picture Archives: 10, 25; Stock Montage, Inc.: 12 right, 24; The Art Archive/Picture Desk/Culver Pictures: 32; The Buffalo News/Robert Kirkham: 19; The Image Works/Topham: 21.

Colorist for illustrations: Dave Ludwig

Library of Congress Cataloging-in-Publication Data

Venezia, Mike.
  Millard Fillmore / written and illustrated by Mike Venezia.
     p. cm.— (Getting to know the U.S. presidents)
  ISBN 0-516-22618-5 (lib. bdg.)   0-516-25487-1 (pbk.)
1. Fillmore, Millard, 1800-1874—Juvenile literature. 2. Presidents—
United States—Biography—Juvenile literature. I. Title.
  E427.V46 2005
  973.6'4'092–dc22

                                   2004022575

A photograph of Millard Fillmore in 1850

Millard Fillmore was the thirteenth president of the United States. He was born on January 7, 1800, in Summerhill, New York. Millard became president during one of the most difficult times in U.S. history. Even though he did a pretty good job, Millard Fillmore is one of the least-remembered presidents.

When Millard Fillmore became president in 1850, the country was having all kinds of problems. These problems were causing Americans to split up into opposing groups.

It seemed like everyone disagreed about almost everything. The biggest problem of all was what to do about slavery. President Fillmore worked as hard as he could to keep the United States together as a country, but it was just impossible to please everyone.

When Millard Fillmore was growing up, no one would ever have guessed that he would be president someday. Millard's parents were extremely poor farmers. They were tricked into buying farmland that was nothing but hard clay and rocks.

Millard hated removing rocks and tree trunks and doing other farm chores. He thought it was very wrong that so many people had to work so hard their whole lives.

The Fillmores' farm couldn't bring in enough money to support the whole family. When Millard was fourteen years old, his father sent him away to be an apprentice at a cloth factory. An apprentice is someone who helps out while learning a job. Mr. Fillmore hoped his son would learn the skills of cloth making and not have to struggle on a farm his whole life.

A replica of Millard Fillmore's birthplace

Millard started out at the factory by carding, or untangling, wool to get it ready to make into cloth. Millard's experience was a bad one, though. He had a terrible boss who was mean and uncaring. Millard's boss almost worked his employees to death.

Millard was apprenticed to a cloth factory like this one.

Millard soon left his job and walked 100 miles (161 kilometers) back to his home. From that day on, Millard Fillmore hated people who treated others unfairly. Millard's father was disappointed when his son returned, but kept looking for a way to help him. In the meantime, a wonderful thing happened. A new school opened near the Fillmores' farm.

This is the type of school Millard attended when he was nineteen.

Millard had just barely learned to read while growing up. He really loved reading, but he had a hard time understanding many of the words he came across. Now, at the age of nineteen, he was excited to have a chance to improve his vocabulary and learn about math, science, and history.

To make things even better, Millard's teacher was just about his age. Her name was Abigail Powers. Millard sometimes had a hard time paying attention in class because he suddenly found himself falling in love with Abigail.

Millard (left) fell in love with Abigail Powers (below).

Abigail was an excellent teacher. She encouraged Millard to do his best at difficult subjects in school. Because of Abigail, Millard realized that he could achieve almost anything he wanted.

During this time, Millard's father arranged for his son to work for a local judge, where he would be able to study law. Millard was thrilled! He decided to become a lawyer. He worked as hard as possible to learn everything he could from the judge.

MILLARD BEFORE MEETING ABIGAIL

MILLARD AFTER MEETING ABIGAIL

Millard then got a job as an assistant in a big law office in the nearby city of Buffalo, New York. He worked on improving his appearance, too. He dumped his farm clothes and began wearing fancy leather shoes and fine suits. He also began carrying a walking stick. Millard wanted to look spiffy for business and for Abigail.

Millard and Abigail lived in this house in East Aurora, New York, in the late 1820s.

Millard learned quickly and soon passed all of his law exams. He became a lawyer in 1823. Millard opened his own law office in the small town of East Aurora, where his parents lived. Three years later, he and Abigail got married.

Millard was well liked and became very successful. Important townspeople enjoyed

stopping by Millard's office to hang out
and chat about news of the day. Someone
suggested that Millard Fillmore should
try to get elected as a New York state
representative. Millard agreed. He entered
the next election, and won!

Millard did a good job as a state representative. He worked hard for the people of his state. He helped pass one law that stopped the state from sending poor people to prison.

In the 1830s, you could be sent to jail if you couldn't pay your bills or didn't pay back money you owed. Millard thought it made

A debtor's prison in the early 1800s

more sense to keep people out of jail so they could keep working. That way, they might eventually be able to pay back their debts. Throughout his life, Millard never forgot how difficult life could be for poor people.

The citizens of New York really liked Millard Fillmore's ideas. In 1832, they elected him to represent their state in the U.S. House of Representatives.

For the next twelve years, Millard Fillmore had a pretty successful political career. Sometimes he would take time off from his elected jobs and return to his law business in Buffalo, New York. Millard and Abigail kept busy working and raising their two children, Millard Powers and Mary. They also helped set up Buffalo's first library.

Millard Fillmore's daughter, Mary Abigail Fillmore

Millard Fillmore was Buffalo's most famous resident. After Fillmore died, the city erected a statue in his honor.

In 1847, Millard ran for an important job called state comptroller. He won the election by so many votes that a political group called the Whig Party became interested in him. Whig leaders thought Millard might be a good choice for vice president in the next national election.

The Whig party had already chosen a
popular war hero named Zachary Taylor as
their presidential candidate. By this time,
the United States was totally divided over
the problem of slavery.

Slaves in the South in the mid-1800s

Most people in the southern states felt it was their right to own slaves. Most people in the northern states thought slavery was wrong. Since Zachary Taylor was from the South and Millard Fillmore was from the North, the Whigs thought they could please people from all over the country.

A campaign handkerchief from the 1840 presidential election

Even though it was a close race, the Whigs' plan worked. In 1848, Zachary Taylor and Millard Fillmore won the election. Unfortunately, Zachary Taylor didn't think much of his vice president. He pretty much ignored Millard's suggestions and left him out of important meetings. President Taylor's closest advisors snubbed the vice president, too.

Millard found himself without much to do. He did have ideas, though, on how to fix the country's slavery problem. Millard agreed with Henry Clay, a famous senator of the time. Henry Clay thought the United States could solve its differences by making some compromises.

Henry Clay

Henry Clay hoped people would agree to a group of new laws he put together. One law suggested that California be admitted to the country as a free state, or a state where slavery wasn't allowed. Another law said that new territories won in the recent Mexican war could make up their own minds about slavery when they became states. Henry also suggested that slaves should no longer be bought and sold in the nation's capital, Washington, D.C. Senator Clay thought these compromises would keep people in the North happy.

Runaway slaves being returned to their masters in the 1850s

To please people in the South, there would be a law that said runaway slaves must be returned to their masters. This law became known as the Fugitive Slave Act. President Taylor wasn't happy with the compromises, though, and said he would reject, or veto, them. Then something happened that no one ever expected!

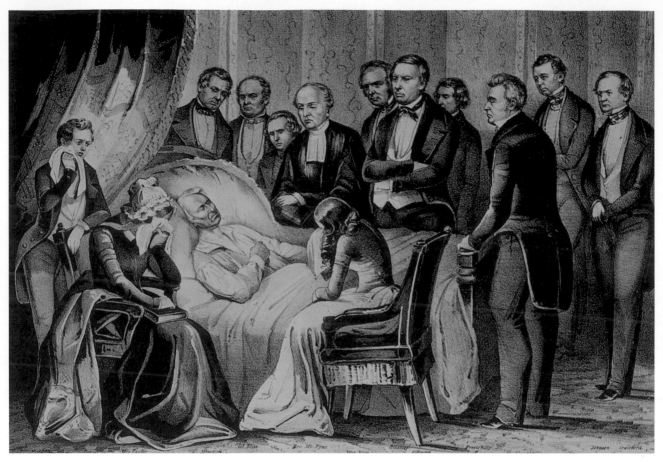

An illustration showing the death of Zachary Taylor

In 1850, during a Fourth of July celebration, President Taylor became very sick with stomach problems. A few days later, the president died. Suddenly, the vice president whom everyone had ignored was in charge of the whole country! Millard Fillmore was as surprised as anyone. He never expected to be president of the United States.

President and Mrs. Fillmore riding in a carriage in 1851

Millard didn't hold a grudge against the people who had treated him badly. Instead, he went to work to do what he thought was best to keep the United States together. President Fillmore signed all of Henry Clay's suggested laws. They became known as The Compromise of 1850.

The Compromise of 1850 did keep the United States from civil war for the next ten years. While trying to make the compromise work, however, President Fillmore made lots of people mad. These people felt forced into accepting things they really didn't believe in.

President Fillmore seemed to have better luck dealing with foreign countries. He sent Commodore Matthew Perry to Japan to see if the government there would start trading goods with the United States.

A Japanese print showing Commodore Perry's ship arriving in Japan in 1853

It was an important change in Asian-American relations. President Fillmore also prevented the Hawaiian Islands from being taken over by the country of France.

In 1850, President Fillmore made another important foreign-policy decision. For a long time, American businessmen had been helping themselves to bird droppings, or guano, that piled up on islands off the coast of Peru. This guano was valuable to American farmers, who used it for fertilizer.

Eventually, the government of Peru objected. It warned American ships to stay away, or else. The businessmen decided

to ignore the order. They asked President Fillmore to send navy ships to protect them.

President Fillmore refused to help the businessmen. He said the United States had no right to take anything from Peru without that country's permission. The Peruvian government was happy to see that the United States respected its rights. President Fillmore's actions also sent a message to other nations that the United States could be trusted.

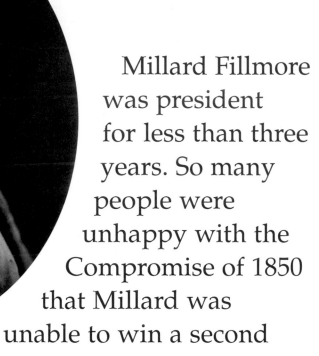

A photograph of Millard Fillmore in the 1860s

Millard Fillmore was president for less than three years. So many people were unhappy with the Compromise of 1850 that Millard was unable to win a second four-year term as president.

Southerners felt the compromise favored the northern states too much. People from the North hated the unfair fugitive slave law. President Fillmore made enemies in the North and South while trying to do what he truly felt was best for his country. When Millard Fillmore died at the age of seventy-four in 1874, hardly anyone seemed to notice.